TAINTED

Tainted

by
Wendy Jett

Accents Publishing • Lexington, Kentucky • 2024

Printed in the United States of America

Accents Publishing
Editor: Katerina Stoykova-Klemer
Cover Art: Stevie Sidney

Library of Congress Control Number: 2024935133
ISBN: 978-1-961127-07-4
First Edition

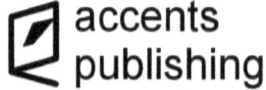
accents
publishing

Accents Publishing is an independent press for brilliant voices. For a catalog
of current and upcoming titles, please visit us on the Web at

www.accents-publishing.com

Contents

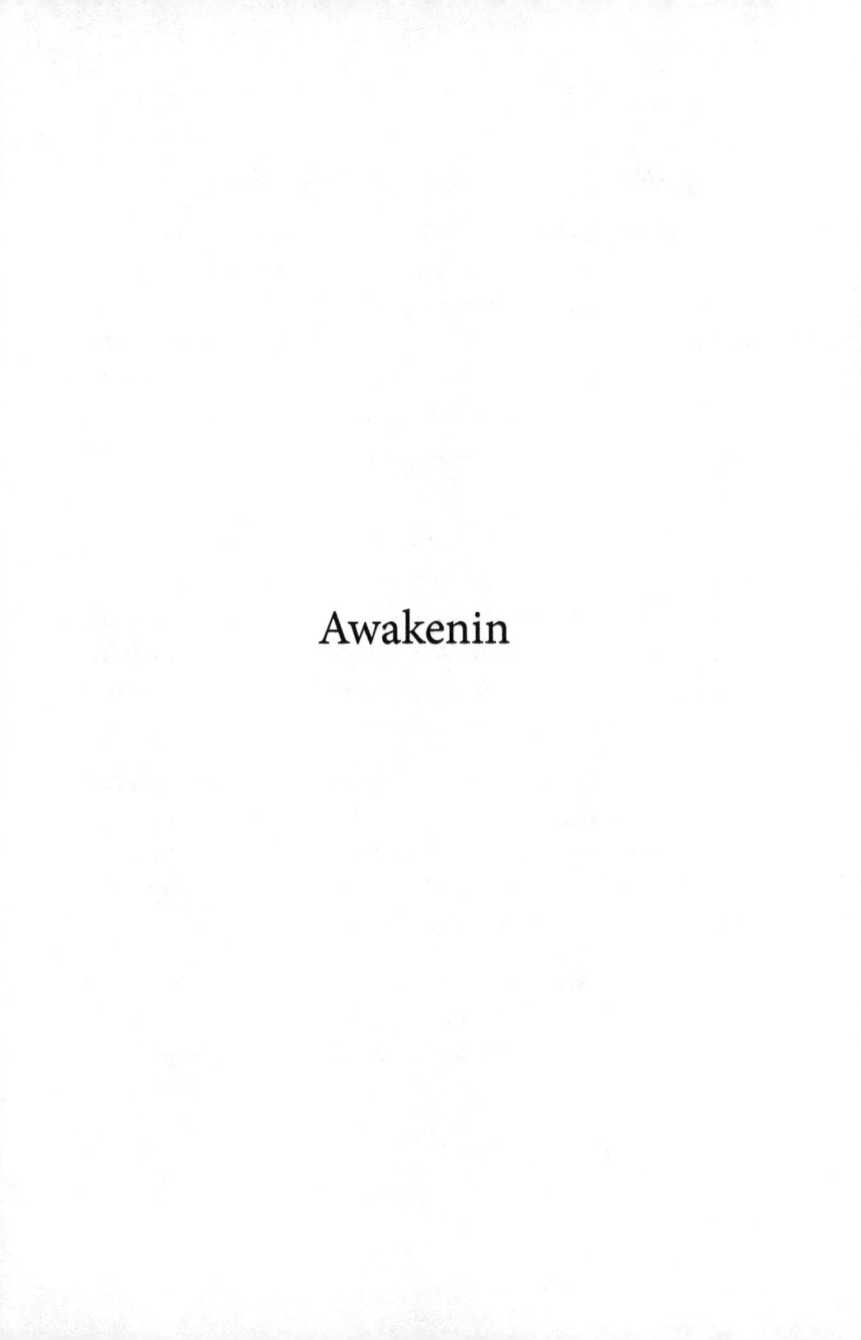

Awakenin

Get up! Get up! I see sumthin! I see sumthin! Get up!

Huckleberry's at the winda barkin like he treed a squirrel. I jump outta bed fast as I can I don't want him wakin Mama. The moon's hangin high like a lightbulb in the black sky. I can see a man standin out there. Next to the big oak. Holdin his hat like a preacher prayin. But it ain't Pastor John. This man has a beard danglin under his chin. Huckleberry starts growlin and clickin his nails on the sill.

Bout that time Mama walks out from under the porch roof. She has her nightshirt on and a wrap round her shoulders. Mama knows better than to go out in the dark with some strange man. What does she think she's doin? I best get Daddy's gun and take Huckleberry with me but I'm too scared to take my eyes offa her.

Looks like Mama's talkin to the man. He puts his hat back on and takes a step to her. Then I see Mama reach out to the man. She holds his hands. They stand there in the moonlight talkin and shakin their heads. Seems like hours fore Mama turns toward the house.

Me and Huckleberry run to the livin room and toss the door open. "Mama, Mama! Come in, Mama!" Huckleberry runs outta the door barkin, toward the man.

You ain't supposed ta be here! You're up ta no good … Nuthin good at all.

Mama yells, "Get back here Huck!" Course Huckleberry turns and runs to Mama. He's a good boy. Mama steps in the door and pulls off her wrap. "You best be gettin back in that bed, Girl tomorra's a school day."

"Who's that man Mama? What's he doin in our yard?" I can't help but look outta the door. He's just standin there at the tree.

"Well, that's your Daddy, Girl. Who you think that is? He's all tore up bout what happened to Petey. He's been visitin him most nights lately. I told him he needs to turn himself over to God and forgive himself. The Lord has already forgivin him."

"Well, I ain't never forgivin him, Mama. I don't care if God wants me to or not. I ain't doin it."

Mama gives me one of them looks she carries inside her eyes. The kind that speaks without sayin no words. Huckleberry steps tween me and Mama. I think he knows them looks too.

"You best be gettin yourself in that bed, Girl, and sayin your prayers. Then you open them ears up nice and wide and listen ta what God whispers back to ya." Mama points to my room and snaps them fingers.

Me and Huck walk to my room. I hear Mama makin her way to her bed. I peek outta the winda. The moon is still high in the sky. There he stands. Next to all his boy babies. Hands a folded like he's prayin. But Daddy never prays.

I hear sumthin tap, tap, tappin on the corner of the winda. Can't be the wind. It's still as a stone out there. Tap tap, tappin. Well, I'll be. It's a dragonfly. Bumpin himself gainst the winda. Tap, tap, tappin, tap, tap, tappin tap, tap, tappin.

she is

an open wound
raw
tender

trauma still seeping

edges
frayed

susceptible to pathogens

of the
heart

• *Wendy Jett*

Bro ken

my grieving heart barks at me a rabid dog
attacks at will tears flesh from my shattered bones
tips its head back howls at each
screaming tear drop
as they leap from the ledge of
my cheek

Switchin

If honey an molasses had themselves a baby, it would be the water in Dry Fork Creek. Thick as molasses, yella like honey and with a sweet smell. Granny Faye always said the smell was from them dragonflies that would skate cross the water. She said they was so happy they smelled like heaven.

I tasted that creek one time. Just one swalla and I tell you, it don't taste like no honey. Tastes like the barn smells after a rain. It ain't nothin I want to taste again. But Dry Fork Creek is the best place round here to catch you a frog. There's frogs as small as the nail on your thumb and toads as big as your hand. Me and BillyWade always take a trip or two down there every summer.

Last time we went to Dry Fork it ended in a battle with Satan himself.

Me and BillyWade and Sissy Jean and Jack Perry all went down to Dry Fork to get us some frogs. Mama said it was ok as long as Huckleberry came along. Course he's a good boy and he loves the creek so that weren't no problem. We got stuck in that mud up to our knees but we caught us four good frogs. We was gonna take them up to Jack's house and play with em a bit.

Well we was laughin and carryin on climbin up the hill behind Jack's place. Sissy Jean can sure tell some funny frog jokes. So we was just cuttin up. Then there he was. Satan himself. Takin up space inside Jack Perry's

Granny's body. She was carryin a switch that had ta have been a mile long. She started a yellin and growlin at us, actin all crazy.

'What kinda evil deeds you chilren been doin down at that creek!' Ain't no good ever come from boys and girls playin in that creek together! You get yourselves up here right now!'

She was wavin that branch like she was on fire! Slappin that switch cross the back of Jack's bare legs a time or two, then BillyWade's legs and cross Sissy Jean's legs and backside. By the time she got to me Huckleberry was a barkin and I weren't gonna take no switchin so I yelled 'Step back Satan!' but that just made her madder. She switched my bare legs all the way up the hill. Every time my feet hit the ground she'd switch me again. I ran all the way home with that frog in my hand and them welts poppin up on my legs.

I came flyin in that front door yellin at Mama that Satan had taken the earthly form and we need to get Daddy's gun. She didn't know what to think when she saw them welts on my bare legs. Bigger than a hornet's sting they was all swelled up.

I told Mama what happened. Showed her the frog and the mud on Huckleberry's legs. We wasn't doin nothin wrong. I told her we was gonna take them frogs back after we played a bit. Mama wiped my legs with some witch hazel and told me to stay there and drink me some milk. She said she'd only be gone a few minutes.

I watched Mama walk out the front door with Huckleberry taggin along. Cross the front yard to the bush at the edge of the drive. She cut herself a big ol switch and she and Huckleberry made their way in the direction of Jack Perry's house. I said me a little prayer, but I wasn't sure whether to pray for Mama or for Granny Perry.

Sissy Jean

How deep is a frog pond?
Knee deep, knee deep

What kinda cake is a frog's favorite?
A Hoppy Birthday cake

What do frogs drink?
Croak A Cola

If a rabbit and a frog have a baby what's it called?
A Ribbit

What kinda frog has horns?
A bull frog

Why was the frog layin there with his feet in the air?
Cause he croaked

• *Wendy Jett*

Say Your Prayers

now i lay me down to sleep
countin blessins countin sheep

one and two three and four
watch over me my sweet lord

thank you for the hills and trees
for my mama and for me

help me to be kind and good
to do the things i know i should

help
me

forgive jack perry's granny
for every time she hit my fanny

but if she pulls another switch
stands there like a granny witch

lord help me to run even faster
so i can get myself right past her

now i lay me down to sleep
countin blessins countin sheep

Ash

BillyWade's got himself a girlfriend. BillyWade calls her Ash, but her given name is Asher Lynn Morgan. I like her just fine. Her mama's a full blood Cherokee. Her daddy is Granny Faye's cousin. They live just past the railroad tracks. Been here bout two years I'd say. Them boys at school tease her bout as much as they tease BillyWade. They call her a granny witch. I told them they best hope she's not a granny witch cause if she is she will turn them into the ugliest spring lizards round here. They just laugh and spit at me.

BillyWade's girls got the prettiest skin. Looks like coffee with a touch of cream. Hair as thick as a horse's mane and as dark as a night cave. She says she looks like her mama's people. I guess I must look like my mama's people. She's says her people lived here in these hills long time fore anybody else was livin here. They lived here when Dry Fork Creek was a river, and even fore there was a railroad. There's not too many of her people left round here. She said they was run off. Don't seem fair to me to git run offa your own land.

Asher's got herself a pet crow. Really, she does. She calls him Koga. That crow follows her everywhere. Sits outside in the tree by the school buildin all day long. He always moves to the playground swing when Asher's out there. He brings her all kinds of presents. Long pieces of string, buttons and even a coin now and then. I wish I had me a pet crow. Ash says the crow has to pick you, you don't get to pick the crow. I'm guessin that crow picked her cause of that coffee skin and black hair. I'd say she's special just like BillyWade and Petey.

Me and BillyWade and Ash walk home from school together most days. Now that BillyWade and his mama, Ms. Verna, are stayin at Granny Faye's house it makes it a lot easier. Mama said it was the right thing to do to let them live there since the place needed lookin after.

We try ta find bottles on the walk home. Johnson's store will pay you good money for a bottle, but the best place to sell one is up in the woods to the Neace brothers. They will take any kinda bottle or jar. Pop bottle, cannin jar they don't care and they pay more than Johnson's. Course Mama would be madder than a skunk if she knew I went up to the Neace place. She says there's trouble brewin up on that hill 24 hours a day. She'd probly make me cut all the firewood and clean out the barn as penance. But a bottle sold means I can save me some money for Mama's birthday present.

I'm not sure what I'm gonna get Mama for her birthday. She ain't been feelin too good lately. She says she's just tired from workin at the store and she still misses Petey. I miss Petey too. Life just ain't the same without him. I asked Ash if her people can talk to angels and people that passed. She said we can make us a special fire one night and talk to Petey. I'm gonna ask him to give Mama a visit for her birthday. She might just feel better after seein him.

• *Wendy Jett*

Giga (Kee-gah)

We have walked this Trail of
Tears in the footprints of our
grandmother's grandmothers.

Our song carried on the crows back
above the tail of smoking flame.
Great Spirit wipe away our tears.

Let us be strong in the silence.

Blood Root

Mother wildflower
Petals tender white
Lucent yellow core
Naps in shade of wood

Mother warrior
Rhizome thick coarse
Potent toxic fiber
Adorns healer's cheek

Rooted Blood

Confession

As God is my witness, Pastor John, I promise you I'm tellin you the truth! Me and BillyWade and Asher was just collectin bottles along Knob Road. We had us a basket of bottles but wanted a few more. I jumped down in the gully longside the road cause we saw two big milk jugs. I was havin trouble gettin back up to the road when I heard them boys.

Charlie Coomer and his buddies, Vance, Carl and Maxie was standin in a big ol circle round Ash and BillyWade. Carl had our basket of bottles. They didn't even know I was down in that gully so I kinda surprised em. Then Charlie said, "Well, well, well if it ain't the Dog Face Girl." Then they all started a barkin at me. I told Charlie, "At least I ain't a horse's ass." Now that made Asher laugh which didn't go over too good with Charlie. He tossed himself a big ol spit ball right at Asher's face and called her a granny witch. BillyWade jumped toward Charlie but Maxie tripped him up and BillyWade landed in the dirt right on his face. Ash helped BillyWade get up. She told them boys they best be gettin along and to give us our basket of bottles back.

Charlie said, "Ain't no granny witch gonna tell me what ta do." Then he told Vance and Maxie to grab her. They got ahold of her arms an was pullin her toward Charlie. I told them to let her go or I was gonna give them somethin to cry about. Charlie said, "Shut up, Girl." Then he pulled Ash's hair so hard she let out a yelp. I could feel myself burnin deep down in my bones. I took one of them milk bottles I had in my hand and threw it hard as I could at Charlie. Hit him square in the belly. Took his breath and he went to the ground. Well, Vance just turned and pushed Ash backwards. She landed on her backside in the road. That's all it took. I swear on my Mama's name, the heavens opened.

Ash's crow, Koga, came a flyin outta the tree and grabbed hold of Vance's hair. Then there was more and more crows comin from who knows where. They was divin outta the air and tearin out hair. Peckin them boys on the face. I do believe one of them grabbed a piece of Charlie's ear. Them boys dropped that basket and started a yellin for their mamas. They took off runnin down that road like rabbits runnin from a hound. Those crows followed em up over the top of the hill cawin and screechin.

Me and BillyWade and Asher picked up our basket and bottles and made our way to Johnson's store to get us some money. When we got there, Charlie and his buddies was sittin there cryin and a bleedin. Tellin my Mama a bold face lie bout what happened. They said we took a switch to their faces and pulled their hair out. I told Mama they was lyin and was no better than a tailed frog. I told her God himself musta sent them crows to help us just like he sent the locust thousands of years ago. God knows a bad groupa boys when he sees one. Then Charlie told Mama I called him a horse's ass and threw that bottle in his belly. I told Mama he was right I did call him a horse's ass cause he is one. Well, Mama didn't like that too much so she sent me down here to see you, Pastor John.

I don't know what you gonna want me to do to make amends about me throwin that bottle and my mouth sayin them things but I was only tellin the truth, just like I'm doin now. The truth is, as God is my witness, Charlie Coomer ain't nuthin but a horse's ass.

• *Wendy Jett*

Jump Rope

Went to the fair—what did I see?
A horse's ass—big as could be

It's the truth—ain't no rumor
The horse's ass—is Charlie Coomer

C - H - A - R - L - I - E
Charlie Charlie big as could be
C - H - A - R - L - I - E
Charlie Charlie big as could be

Once Upon a Time in
The Land of Ooopapadow

Crow and Dragonfly were
traveling down the road
When along came a little
green hopping toad.

Toad said "Oh my dear
I can't believe my eyes!
I always thought starling
crows ate dragonflies!"

"Silly Toad that's a myth"
cawed the walking crow
"Just a lie to cause unrest
you should let it go."

Dragonfly said to Crow,
"But I have heard it's true
That crows do eat dragonflies
and frogs can eat them too."

Crow tipped back his head
cleared his screechy voice
"Life is just a journey
of making your own choice.

You can choose to be a friend
choose to be a foe
Choose to see the thunder clouds
or the bright rainbow.

I would rather have a friend
than a tasty treat.
Belly full but empty heart
is quite bittersweet.

So let's go friends down this road
standing side by side
A Crow a Frog a Dragonfly
we're all the same inside."

The End

Sundays

Sundays are supposed to be a day of rest, well that's what the Good Book says, but me and Mama are always real busy on Sundays. We get up early and make food for the church supper. Then we stop and say a prayer at the boys grave fore we head off to church. After church supper we always stop at Sister Garnetta's house to check on her and leave her a supper plate. She and Granny Faye were best friends for life. Mama says we need to watch over Sister Garnetta since she ain't got any kin. Never married, no children. Then we stop and visit with Granny Faye and Grandpap. They're buried in the family cemetery next to the blackberry bushes. Sumtimes we leave them some wildflowers. But things just aren't the same round here right now. Mama's not feelin too good.

I didn't think Mama could get any skinnier than after Petey's passin, but I was wrong. She's just a walkin sack of bones right now. Doc Andrews says them cancer drugs will either save her or kill her. We just have to be patient and have faith it will work.

Mama needs to rest on Sundays so we've been stayin home from church. Pastor John's been stoppin by after the service. Mama always seems to feel better after his visit. I think them warm biscuits he brings probly help too. Mama says it ain't proper to listen in on people's conversations with vessels of the Lord so I just sit on the porch while Mama visits with Pastor.

I like sittin on the porch. Sometimes I pretend Petey's

sittin with me. We count the swallas in the yard and play 'I Spy', then we find us a smooth, round rock in the dirt. Clean it up good and put it on the porch. Rocks remind us we are part of this earth and stronger than we think we are. There must be 30 rocks on the stoop now. Mama says the porch looks like a creek bed.

I ain't been to the creek much lately. Don't really wanna leave Mama that long, but sumtimes I sneak down there with Huckleberry while she's nappin. We stay just long enough to get our feet wet and float some leaf boats. Huckleberry always gets himself a good, long drink at the creek.

Been missin my Granny Faye and Grandpap a lot lately. Mama says they are still round us and we can talk to them anytime. But it just ain't the same as sittin with Granny or walkin the fields with Grandpap. Sumtimes I feel like I'm the only person on this earth. Mama says loneliness is grief's shadow. She says the best thing ta do to defeat loneliness is ta get out in the sun or even the moonlight. To close my eyes and take good, deep breaths of air.

I don't know what I'm gonna do if Mama's cancer drugs don't work. Moonlight and deep breathin won't help me thru that. Walks in the woods and hymns won't help me thru that. I been talkin to God bout it, but ta be truthful, he ain't said one word back ta me. Maybe he's feelin lonely too.

• *Wendy Jett*

Mourning Has Broken

gray blue sky   nuzzles   curve of forest green hill
silhouette of black pine   a dark hole in the horizon
gentle drip   of remnant rain   swells   falls from
kudzu leaves   twisted   round and round   round
and round   melancholy swarms   bees on honeycomb

crow caws

there is no
goodnight

The Final Dose

too acidic to swallow

loneliness slid
under her skin
searching for

a vein.

Cartwheelin

I never saw Granny Faye turn a cartwheel fore. She sure can keep them legs straight! Don't seem to mind that her skirt turned up over her head for a second. And boy oh boy that old girl can run fast! I can hardly keep up with her!

The butterfly field is the best place to turn cartwheels. Those butterflies just jump right up outta the grass and dance round your legs! Granny likes the orange ones best. Says they remind her of the sun settin over the hill. I like the black ones with the yella spots. They look like the night sky with the moon sittin in the middle.

Me and Granny been cartwheelin and spinnin circles all mornin. I just been countin the minutes fore we can get in that picnic basket! Granny said she brought fried chicken and cold tater cakes. She said she even made peanut butter fudge! Grandpap always said that when Granny gets to the pearly gates, God himself will ask her for a piece of her fudge! It's that good.

We tied all them little flowers from the clover together and made us a crown and a necklace. Granny says we both look like Queens of the county fair.

Seems like a perfect day to me. Sky so blue you want to dip your toes in it. All them butterflies scattered cross the field wavin to the heavens. Warm breeze floatin through my hair. Granny laughin and twirlin. Them tater cakes sittin in the basket. The only thing that would make it better is if Petey was here.

Granny picks up the picnic basket and starts a runnin toward the creek. "C'mon Girl, let's eat on the other side!" She looks just like a deer leapin cross those rocks in the creek. Feet barely touchin down fore she's on another. "C'mon Girl, ain't you hungry?" Granny starts wavin.

I start runnin fast as I can. I know them tater cakes are gonna be good. But I get to the edge of the creek and just stop. Sumthin tells me I shouldn't cross that creek. That little voice in my heart is tellin me I won't be able to git back if I cross them rocks.

Granny just smiles, "Don't chew wanna play no more Girl?"

"I'm scared Granny. I'm scared I won't be able to see Mama again if I cross that creek."

"It's ok Girl. I love you. I'll come and play with you again sumtime. You take care of your Mama. Keep givin her that tea and broth!" Granny waves and starts walkin cross the field.

"Don't go Granny, don't go!" I don't want Granny to leave! I want to cartwheel and eat that fudge with her. Granny is gettin smaller and smaller. The sun sure is bright. Bouncin right off that water into my eyes. It's blindin. I can't see Granny no more.

I hear Mama pullin back them curtains. "Git up Girl, we got chores this Saturday mornin! Sky's so blue you will wanna dip your toes in it! I'm feelin pretty good today, let's have us a picnic!"

Granny Faye's Tater Cakes

2 cups mashed taters from night before
1 cup flour
1 egg
2 pinches pepper
2 pinches salt (and maybe one pinch more)
1 onion smaller than palm of your hand
3 handfuls chopped cheese
left over cooked bacon or sausage
oil or fat or butter

Chop up the onion, you can cut it in a bowl of cold water and then drain the water if the onion is makin you tear up but don't be touchin your eyes (wash your hands after)

Use a big bowl mix mashed taters, flour, egg, onion, pepper, and salt in a bowl until it looks like cake batter

Then stir in your cheese and bacon. Mix it real good.

Heat up the oil or fat or butter in a skillet til it's hot.

Use a big spoon to get the batter and drop it in the skillet. Don't let it spatter.
Smash it down just a touch.

When the tater cake turns brown, flip it over to the other side.

When it's done take it out of the skillet and put it on a towel for a minute to drain.

You can eat tater cakes with butter, syrup, honey, molasses, tiger sauce, or sugar on top.

But the best thing to eat them with is Granny's mustard.

Granny's Heavenly Peanut Butter Fudge

2 pinches salt
2 cups sugar
¾ cup milk

stir it
boil all this to a soft ball feelin

this means you hafta have a coffee cup of water by the stove then you drop a bit of this in the water and feel around in there to see if it makes a soft ball if it doesn't then keep tryin be careful you don't burn yourself the hot sugar will stick to your skin

take it off the heat and hurry to stir in
1 tea vanilla
1 cup marshmallow creme
1 cup peanut butter

pour in buttered dish
after it sets up cut it into squares
you can make a lot and freeze some if you want

Afflictions

'Mama's dyin. Mama's dyin. Your mother is dying.' The only thing worse than hearin them words is the fact they are comin outta my Daddy's mouth. Daddy walks down the porch steps and past me on the front walk.

I run up the steps and hollar, "I know Mama's dyin. Who you thinks been lookin after Mama all these months? Helpin her button her blouse so she can crawl her way to work. Fixin her chicken broth and steamin tea. I can tell you it ain't been you, Daddy."

Daddy turns to me but don't say a word.

"I've heard them stories bout you takin up with Loretta Thompson. Everybody's been talkin bout you and your selfish way of livin. Me and Mama don't want no part of you. You best be gettin yourself right back up that hill. And don't be tellin us your heart's broke."

Daddy's face changes color. I've seen that color fore, many a time. Them seeds are bein sown. I step back toward the front door. Daddy moves to me and stops. Daddy says, "Watch your mouth, Girl. I'm still your Daddy."

Bout that time Mama opens the front screen. Steps out with a hat in her hand. Huckleberry comes runnin out. "Here ya go." She passes the hat to Daddy. "What you two been talkin bout out here?"

Daddy says, "I was just tellin my Girl here what a good job she's bein doin carin for you and all."

I can feel my face changin color. I can feel them roots growin down in my bones. "That's a bold face lie. You never said them words. You never said nuthin like that."

Mama turns to me, grabs me by the hand. "Now try to mind your manners Girl. Don't be talkin to your Daddy that way. Why don't you go on inside and rustle me up some of that steamin tea and honey you're so good at fixin. Your Daddy's leavin."

I tell Huckleberry to com'on. but he just sits on the porch next to Mama. The screen slams behind me. I turn back to see my Daddy put his hat on and give a tip of his head to Mama. Daddy says, "I'll be back to check on you soon woman. You take care of yourself. You gotta get that girl under control. She's a wildcat that one is." Then he just walks off cross the yard past the big Oak.

Mama stands there still as a stone and watches Daddy til he goes up and over the hill at the end of the drive. I hear Mama say, "Huck, I know that man carries trouble in his pocket, but God help me, I still love him."

Nuthin goods gonna come from that. Nuthin good at all.

Satan is sowin seeds. Seeds are takin root. Them roots are goin deep.

• *Wendy Jett*

Tea Time

fill kettle with hope
nestle on hot stove

drop one tea bag
in cup of faith

when kettle sings
pour hope into faith

add 2 teaspoons sweet courage
stir gently with love

Bereavement

Grief floods over me
I cannot stay afloat
It pulls me deeper
I lay at the bottom
I can only look up
Dim light at the surface
There you are looking down at me

|
|
|
|
|
|
|
|
|

Looking down at me there you are
At the surface dim light
Look up only I can
At the bottom I lay
Deeper it pulls me
Afloat I cannot stay
Over me grief floods

Covenant

Huck, I don't know what I'm gonna do if Mama don't get better. I try not to think of them things but sumtimes they just creep inta my heart. I can tell you this, we ain't gonna live with Daddy if Mama passes. We can catch us a train right outta here and figure things out on our own. What do you think of that Huck? You awake?

My Girl seems to be frettin over sumthin. I can always tell by the way her cheeks taste all salty. I know Mama ain't been feelin too good. We been makin her lots of tea and I been takin lots of naps with her most days.

You gotta move over a bit Huck. I can't get them covers pulled right. You awake boy?

Ain't nothin good gonna come from Daddy visitin Mama. Nuthin good at all. I heard them tales bout Daddy and Daisy. I heard them tales bout Daddy and Petey.

That's a good boy. Move on over. You know your lips stuck on that lil tooth again, don't cha? Here let me fix that for you. Scooch a little closer Huck. I think maybe me and you need ta make a swear. Like a blood bond swear but without the blood. I don't know how dogs make a blood bond swear but let's just make us a swear. I ain't gonna let nuthin bad happen to you and you ain't gonna let nuthin bad happen to me. We gotta stick together Huck. Me and you. We ain't got no more family besides Mama. Daddy ain't family. I know Mama says he is, but I think Mama ain't thinkin right with that cancer in her body.

I love when my Girl looks in my eyes. I can see that little flame down in the middle of her spirit. It's still there, it's just a little harder to see these days. I think the world is tryin to put that flame out. But I ain't gonna let it. I ain't gonna let nuthin bad happen to my Girl. Her little heart's broke and it's just gonna take some time for it to heal.

Sumtimes I think I hear Petey out in the yard. Laughin and chasin them crickets. But he ain't never there. Mama says it's them angels givin me a sign that he's doin ok. Maybe chasin some crickets in heaven. I don't know what to think these days. There's days I don't even wanna be here on this earthly plain. Do you ever feel like that Huck? Mama says everybody feels like that sumtimes. Specially when you lost someone you love. Grief can be a heavy coat to wear. Mama says I should't cry for yesterday, or worry bout tomorrow. She says we need our strength to get through the day we are in. I know Mama's right, but my heart does what it wants most days.

My Girl smells like fresh grass and mint tea tonight. I don't even hafta take a deep breath. I can smell the softness of the grass in her hair. But I can tell by the way she's breathin she's feelin a lonely tonight so I'm gonna snuggle a bit closer. She likes it when I lay my head on her chest. I like it too. My Girl starts hummin a hymn. I know its a hymn cause I heard Mama sing it to her many a time. She takes a quick little breath now and then to keep that hum flowin.

I think we should go up to McClure's farm tomorra Huck. Just me and you. We can do that while Mama's nappin. I always feel better layin up under them pine trees. I love you Huck. Night boy.

I love you my Girl. Sleep tight. I will be right here.

• *Wendy Jett*

Grief

plucks his pale gray suit coat
from hanger | clenches
fist | thrusts through satin lined
sleeve | breast pocket cradles
frayed yellowed handkerchief |
slate tie squeezes adam's

apple | smooths wrinkles along
seam of pant leg | black
scuff mark on shoe
disappears under sliding
thumb | labored steps | shoves
door open | air too thick
to lift the crows | smells like rain

God Said

I will send my kindest
angels to comfort them.
Send only those that truly
understand unconditional
love. They will provide
support during hard times.
Patience during trying times.
Laughter and a sense of joy
daily. Their wings will be
transformed into paws. Feet
and legs strong enough to carry

the weight of a huge heart.
They will be loyal, loving and
forgiving. They will replenish
their spirits quickly with short
naps and long walks. They will
soak in the sun and howl at the
moon. Reminding all to appreciate
each day and night together.
Although their lifespan will not be

long, their impact will be unforgettable.
I will give them my name to remind
them that I am always there beside them.

The doG will be my ambassador, my earthly angel.

Liar Liar

I lied to Mama twice today. Two whole times. I knew I was lyin when I did it but I did it anyway. She asked me why I smelled like cigarettes. I told her BillyWade smoked a cigarette he found on the stoop at Johnson's store and I was with him. Which is true, but I left out the part about me smokin a cigarette too. So maybe that was just half a lie or maybe just a fib. But when she asked me where we was when he smoked it, I told her a big lie. I said we was just sittin on the tree stump by the creek. We wasn't, we was sittin right in the middle of the Green River Railroad Bridge. It would break Mama's heart if she knew I was up on that bridge. So I lied. A big fat lie.

Green River Railroad Bridge is the highest rail bridge in the whole state. Nobody's supposed to walk on that bridge cause it's too hard to get cross if a train starts round the bend. There ain't no room to stand on that bridge and let it pass. Peoples jumped offa that bridge many a times over the years tryin to get away from that train. Most of em died. Either had a heart attack on the way down, or drown in that river. That's the river Granny Faye's daddy drown in. The water under that bridge swirls in circles and sumtimes even squares. It will suck you right under into Satan's den. There's even been people that jumped offa there on purpose to end their own life. They just couldn't take all the earthly worries they was carryin.

Me and BillyWade and Ash been up there three times

now. First time I was too scared to go out on the bridge. Me and Huck just stayed there on the ground worryin bout BillyWade and Ash. But Ash said Koga would tell us if that train was a comin. So I sat there til a train came just to see if she was right and she was. Koga started a sqawkin and flappin his wings fore that train even came round that bend. They didn't have no trouble gettin offa that bridge in time.

The last two times we been up there I went out on the bridge. What a glorious sight it is! The dancin river, miles of trees reachin for the clouds with little clearins where a house pops up. Puffs of smoke comin up from the sawmill. The crows soarin down to dip their beaks in the water. It truly is amazin. That bridge sure gets you closer to heaven just standin on it. If there's a perfect place to choose to die, it's probly there.

Today we sat right in the middle of that bridge danglin our legs over. Huck wouldn't even come out on it. Stayed up there on the ground, layin in the dirt. We smoked us a cigarette, just cause. Didn't really care for it. My mouth tasted all dirty after. BillyWade tossed the resta that pack offa the bridge. We counted to 16 fore it hit the water.

Ash said she would just turn into a bird and fly away if she fell offa that bridge. BillyWade said he would just drown cause he ain't a very good swimmer. I think maybe my Granny Faye would catch me if I fell off, but I didn't tell them that. I just kept it to myself. We laid back on that bridge and watched the clouds wiggle themselves into the shapes of animals. There was a horse, a long tailed fish, a mama bear and even a fat dragonfly. BillyWade said God was paintin for us. I think that might be true.

I really don't like lyin to Mama. I know it's not the proper thing ta do, but sumtimes you just hafta protect other people's hearts from breakin by lyin just a bit. I never usta lie, not really. Seems like I'm not myself lately. Lyin and smokin cigarettes sounds like sumthin my Daddy might do. I know I got some of my Daddy's bones in me but I'm prayin I got more of my Mama.

Tongue on Fire

when she

Opens
her mOuth
wOrds

singe
her
lips

plume
of charcoal
smoke
jettisons

to her mOther's ear
s e e p s into her bOdy
scOrches her heart

• *Wendy Jett*

Thinkin

1. Was
2. it
3. a
4. fall
5. or
6. a
7. jump
8. or
9. a
10. push?
11. In
12. the
13. end
14. it
15. didn't
16. matter.

Harken

Me and Mama been snappin beans all mornin. Ta tell ya the truth, my fingers are plum wore out. But I'm not gonna tell Mama that. She needs the help. Ever once in a while I toss Huck a bean. He usually plays with it a bit fore he eats it. He loves all kinda food from the garden. I think beans and carrots are his favorite. He's a good boy.

Mama went in to get us sumthin to snack on. It's too early for supper but my belly is a growlin. The wind is blowin just enough to hear them angels whisperin in the woods. Mama says they are talkin bout the storm that's supposed to be comin tomorra. I don't care for storms, but Mama loves em. She sits right on the porch and watches the lightnin and smells the rain. She says storms wash away all the world's evil deeds. After the storm the world gets ta start over. Kinda like bein baptized. She says them storms nourish the earth and cleanse its core. I try to sit on the porch with her when it rains, but if it's lightnin, I gotta get inside. It sends a chill up my arms. All them little hairs stand up like a whistle pig in the field.

Huck's tail starts a waggin so I know Mama's makin her way to the door. *Mama's comin Mama's comin, she's got cornbread!* She has a big tray so I hop up and open the door for her. It's cornbread, a pitcher of buttermilk and two glasses. Mama says, "I thought we could have us some of Petey's favorite food. Moo Mush. "Well, that's what Petey called it when he was real little. You take some day old cornbread and crumble it up in the glass. Pour some cold buttermilk over it and eat it with a spoon. It's like a taste of heaven in your mouth. I'm glad Mama's eatin some with me, she's skinny as a cattail right now.

Mama says, "Girl, I'm worried bout you. You just haven't been yourself at all lately. I know Petey's passin has been a load to carry, but you don't hafta carry that all by yerself." Mama sits her mush down and starts snappin a few beans.

I tell her, "I'm doin fine Mama. You don't need to worry bout me." I get me a big bite of mush and feel that cold buttermilk run down my chin. Mama takes her apron and wipes it away for me.

"Tastes pretty good, don't it?" Mama picks her mush back up and takes her a spoonful. "You've had a lot of loss in your young life, Girl. Granny Faye, Grandpap, Petey and Daisy. There's many a grown people that haven't had that much loss in their lives yet. And now with me being sick, I think maybe you're feelin mad bout it all."

I don't look at Mama. I just stare down in my milk. I don't wanna talk bout Petey leavin, or Granny Faye or nobody. I don't like the way I feel when I think bout it. I don't say nothin.

Mama says, "Now it might be hard to talk bout, Girl, but I'm your Mama, you can always talk to me bout things. I love you no matter what. Ain't nuthin in the world that would make me stop lovin you. Nuthin." Mama's glass is empty so she puts it down and picks up some beans. "You know when you lose someone you love, like Petey, there's a little hole in your soul where they usta take up space. You need ta work hard at fillin that hole back up with good things. Things like happy memories. Prayers. Sunshine. Hymns. Friends. They can all help fill that space. If ya don't fill it with good things, the bad things in the world will jump right in that hole. Things like gettin mad bout everythin, talkin sassy, lyin, not sleepin, eatin or drinkin too much. Satan has a way of knowin where those holes are and he will just jump right in there."

I swalla the last drop of that Moo Mush and pick me up some beans. Start snappin em hard. I don't like what Mama's talkin bout. I feel myself burnin inside.

"Now I know you might not wanna talk bout this. But I'm worried bout you, Girl. You been yellin and gettin mad at the drop of a hat. Been lyin to me bout where you been. That's not like you. I want to help you fill them holes with the good so the bad can't get in. I bought you a present." Mama stands up and goes inta the house.

I look at Huck. He's just sleepin. He don't even see that crow standin out there in the yard.

Mama comes outta the house with sumthin in her hand. She hands me a new, thick notebook of paper. It has drawings of dragonflies on the front cover. She gives me four new pencils and a pencil sharpener. The kind you can carry in your pocket.

Mama says, "Now I want you to use this little book to write down anythin you want to. I won't be a readin it. Nobody will. But if you get mad bout sumthin, come write it in your book. You can be as mean as you want to in this book. Write it all down. Get it all outta your body. You can even draw you some pictures if you want to. It's your book." Mama picks some beans up and dumps em in her lap. She starts snappin. "After you get all that meanness out on that paper, I want ya to write one good thing down. Sumthin you love bout the world. It could be your friend's name, or the creek rocks, or even Huck's funny little front tooth. Anythin in the world that makes you feel good. Do you think you can do that for me, Girl?"

I look up at Mama. She's smilin with her eyes. I tell her, "Yes ma'am, I can do that. Thank you Mama."

Mama says, "Grab you a string and let's tie up the resta these beans and make us some leather britches. I know they are your favorite."

Notebook

i can hear them
hills a cryin

there's just too
many good people
buried in their bellies

i hear you cryin
oh my hills

i be cryin with you

Notebook

my cup is
FULL
to the brim with

emptiness

Ambush

"Hey, ain't that your daddy?" Ash points tween the leaves on the bushes. We been sittin here bout a hour waitin for Charlie Coomer to come by. We got a plan to put him in his place for once and all. I poke my eye through the openin. Sure nuf it's my Daddy and my Mama. I see BillyWade on the other side of the road poke his finger outta the bush. He sees em too. I guess we ain't gonna be able to give Charlie his due. "Wanna say hi?" Asher shrugs at me. "No no no" I whisper, "Keep quiet."

What are they doin walkin down here together? Mama must be on her break from the store. They're walkin right down the middle of the road holdin hands. I can't believe it. She's holdin his hand. The hand that struck her like lightnin. Mama should be restin on her work break, not walkin with Daddy. Ain't any reason to walk with Daddy that I can think of.

I can feel myself gettin hot. Sweat beads startin on my back. I don't like what I'm seein. Maybe I should ask Ash to send Koga down on Daddy. Peck his eyes out or just scare the life outta him. He'd deserve it. Yes he would. Mama would say I'm lettin Satan in with those thoughts. Maybe so, I don't know. These days I seem to be swayed by Satan.

Well here comes Huck trottin up behind em. He musta caught wind of us cause he's lookin this way. Go away Huck. Don't be comin over here. He raises his nose and starts ta mosey over.

I smell my Girl here. I know I do. What's she doin in the bush?

"Git, git Huck." I whisper but he just keeps comin. Bout that time, Mama stumbles knees to ground. Huck runs over and Daddy pulls her back up.

"I'm ok. I'm just tired. I should go back to the store. C'mon Huck." Mama turns back and Daddy puts his arm round her. They all head back toward Johnson's. We just watch em till they top the little knob in the road.

"Why didn't cha wanna talk to your mama?" Ash steps outta the bush. "She woulda been happy to see ya I'm sure." BillyWade crosses over the road. "She just don't wanta see her daddy," he says with a smirk. "Me either. That man don't care for me much."

Here comes clangin long the road, it's Charlie Coomer and Maxie. Ridin them rusty old bikes of theirs. Gravel flyin up round them. "Well if it aint the Granny Witch, the Dog Face Girl and Prissy Boy. All the freaks together I see." Charlie stops his bike and spits in our direction. Maxie starts circlin us on his bike.

"Go on get outta here Charlie. I think I see some crows sittin in them trees up ahead." BillyWade laughs and points. Charlie and Maxie start barkin and take off up the road. Ash says, "Go on Koga." Koga takes off flyin up the road right over top of Charlie and Maxie. Dippin down every once in a while just ta give em a scare.

BillyWade says, "Hey looky there!" He points down to the toe of my sneaker. A dragonfly.

Notebook

Mama, go tell the songbird today ain't for singin.
Mama, go tell the trout lily today ain't for bloomin.
Mama, go tell the holler winds today ain't for blowin.
Mama, go tell the red tailed hawk today ain't for soarin.

Mama, today ain't the day. Mama, today ain't the day.
Mama, today ain't the day. Mama, today ain't the day.
Mama, today ain't the day. Mama, today ain't the day.
Mama, today ain't the day. Mama, today ain't the day.

Notebook

Lightnin struck her
but she ain't cryin.

She just holds it in her hand
And walks down the road with it.

Mama a storm is a brewin.

Revival

It's so hot you can hear your sweat sizzle when it hits the ground … and let me tell you, there's a lot of sweatin goin on in that tent. I think everyone in the county is here. It is a sight to see and some terrible smells to smell. All them people sweatin and hollerin and dancin makes for a smell worse than Mama's fried liver-n-onions.

Revivals are bout as big as Christmas round here. Lots of food and music and singin. The Holy Spirit always has a way of makin itself known. One year the whole tent fell on top everybody. Wind just took the poles right outta the ground, but everybody just kept singin and praisin the Lord. Pastor John said it was the best revival he ever saw, but I think this year's gonna outshine that one.

Mama always goes to the revivals but this one is most special. Pastor John has a travelin preacher comin in. Brother Thomas. He's a preacher and a healer. He can lay his hands on the sick and heal em right there and then. Mama and Ms. Verna got here early to have a front row seat. Mama's startin to look pekid from the heat, but she says she's doin ok. Me and BillyWade and Asher are gonna stay outta that tent til it's healin time. We just can't take the heat and smell no more.

We hear a big ol commotion comin up the road. There's people runnin and whistlin and clappin. It's the travelin preacher walkin up the drive. Dust kickin up under his feet and hat on his head. I have to tell you, he is the most beautiful man I ever seen. Eyes as blue as the sky and teeth as white as the snow. Eyelashes so long there's a breeze every time he blinks. He has his suit coat tossed over his shoulder so you can see them black suspenders he's a wearin. BillyWade says Pastor Thomas looks just like Jesus himself walkin down the road. I'm sure I smelled fresh honeysuckle when he walked past us.

Brother Thomas stops and gets himself a good long drink at one of the food tables, then he goes straight in the tent to start spreadin the gospel. People just start hollerin and stompin their feet the second he steps in there. Somebody has themself a tambourine, starts shakin it so fast it sounds like the tent roof is gonna split wide open. It's a good thing Mama and Ms. Verna have themselves a seat. There ain't hardly any room for us to squish in.

Just like that, everybody starts singin *There is Power in the Blood*. Stompin and clappin. Roberta Johnson starts a twirlin round and round so fast I think I saw both her feet lift offa the ground. Pastor John is singin loud as can be. Slappin his legs like they are on fire!

Brother Thomas raises his hands to the heavens and asks the Lord to bring forth those that need healin. Mama stands up. That tambourine is a shakin, Ms. Verna is a shoutin. Brother Thomas puts his hands right on Mama and she starts a swayin. I can feel the sweat slidin down my back. Mama's eyes are rollin round. My ears start ringin and the room starts a spinnin. I can't breathe. Seems like the tent is gettin smaller and smaller.

Brother Thomas is usin his handkerchief to wipe my face. He's so close I can see the sweat beads on the end of them long lashes. I see his mouth movin but I don't hear nuthin but my heart beatin. Then I see Mama over me. "Girl, you ok? Girl, talk to me honey!" Mama sounds scared. "You just fainted right there. Scared me ta death. Girl, answer me."

I hear myself sayin, "Is this heaven?"

Brother Thomas says, "Well, Girl, that depends on who you ask." He gives me a wink and I feel my hair wave in that eyelash breeze.

Preachin

brothers and sisters i say brothers and sisters we have come together to praise our heavenly father lord we stand before you today with open hearts we humbly pray that you will forgive us for all the ways we have wandered away from your teachins we ask that the holy spirit fills us today lord with faith and healin power help us to be strong against earthly temptations we need your grace your grace your patience lord bring to us your shinin light to cast away the darkness that seems to be hidin down in our hearts lord we lift our arms to you god our father and ask that you draw us closer to you open the eyes of those that have not been able to see your grace and love restore us lord shower us with your mercy there is nothin that is impossible with you no nothing lord nothinnothinnothinthatisimpossiblewithyou father you are mighty you have shown us miracles in healin the sick partin the waters raisin the dead from their graves lord yes raisin yes I say raisin raisinthedeadfromtheirgraves we open our hearts to your words to your ways brothers i say brothers lift your hearts to god almighty sisters i say sisters open your arms and embrace his spirit oh lord heavenly father praise we praise you save the lost heal the sick bring the power of your love and mercy into this place today lord heavenly lordohlord we believewe believe we know you are here with us oh lord lift us up

Notebook

i
drown
myself
in
your
ocean
eyes

dive
deep
into
the
dark
black
center
cave

a
secret
tunnel
into
who
you
are

Birthday

I can smell that pork fat from the front yard. It hangs inside my nose like a beautiful fog of flavor. I love when Mama cooks brown beans and cornbread. She always saves the best little piece of pork fat for me. Sumtimes I sneak me a piece of butter. Just a slice all by itself. Heaven on your tongue I'd say.

Today's Mama's birthday. We been collectin bottles for weeks now. Tryin to save up nuf money to get her a dragonfly necklace from the store catalog. Ms. Verna said she would go pick it up from Johnson's store so Mama won't know a thing bout it.

Ms. Verna, BillyWade and Ash are comin over for Mama's birthday supper. Ms. Verna's bringin her famous Stack cake. She won first prize and fifty dollars for her cake at the county fair last year. Best part of that cake is the apple butter all stuffed tween them layers. Oozes right out when you get you a big bite. Sumtimes a plump ol blob will just plop right down on the floor. Take your breath away, I'd say. I hope she remembers some birthday candles.

Mama's looking awful pretty today. She don't look sick at all. She's lookin like a fresh flower dancin in the sun as she sets the table. Mama says, "We gotta set us an extra bowl and plate, Girl. Your Daddy's comin to eat supper with us."

I can feel the room heatin up with them words. "Your Daddy's comin to eat supper with us." Nuthin goods gonna come from that I'd say. Nuthin good at all.

Course Daddy's the first at the door. I'm guessin he wants sum time with Mama. I wish Ms. Verna, BillyWade and Asher would get here soon. There seems to be lots of foot stompin goin on from my Girl. Door slammin and rattlin of the spoons on the table.

Mama says, "Now mind your manners. It's my birthday after all. Everyone needs to get along today. I got me some good news for my birthday. Y'all just sit down and let me tell you what Doc Andrews told me yesterday."

Chairs scoot out from the table. I try to sit close to Mama and stay away from Daddy. He's up to no good I'd say.

Mama don't sit, she's standin at the top of the table. Smilin with her eyes. "Doc says my cancer's gone! Them cancer drugs did their job. Yes they did! I gotta keep watch on it, but for now, I ain't got cancer!"

I feel my heart a racin and hear everybody else's hearts a thumpin. Daddy jumps up and slaps his hands together! "Hot Damn woman, that's the best birthday present I ever heard of!" He grabs Mama to give her a big squeeze.

Then I see it. Outta the corner of my eye. That butterknife shinin in the sun. Fore I can get up, my Girl has that knife in her hand. Fingers all wrapped round the handle. She starts wavin that knife round, yellin at Daddy. "I'm tellin ya Mama, a snake can shed its skin but it's still a snake! You get yer hands offa my Mama!" My Girl starts a runnin toward Daddy. Mama steps tween them and grabs the knife.

"I told ya ta mind your manners Girl. You go wash up and get

ready for your friends to come over." Mama puts the knife in her apron.

My Girl screams louder than a skinned cat. Her eyes are all bugged out. "I hate you. You ain't my Daddy! I won't never pick a man like you to be my Daddy. You ain't my Daddy! You ain't nuthin but a snake!"

Well Daddy ain't too happy bout them words that come outta her mouth. He pushs Mama outta the way and slams his hand on the table. "Watch your mouth, Girl. I am your Daddy."

My Girl just turns and runs straight outta that front door. Kickin up dirt cross the yard. Mama yells at me, "Go with her Huck! Go!" I take off fast as I can. She's already got a headstart on me.

She ain't runnin to the creek, My Girl is runnin in the direction of that railroad bridge. Nuthin goods gonna come from that I'd say. Nuthin good at all.

Notebook

How To Build A Bean's Nest
1. Simmer brown beans on hot stove til pork fat hangs in the air
2. Bake skillet cornbread til crunchy
3. Chop onion on counter (don't be touchin your eyes)
4. Crumble warm cornbread into deep bellied bowl
5. Plop beans
6. Sprinkle onion
7. Add dribble of milk from your glass
8. Time to pray

They Sewed Her Lips Together
With Each Remark A Stitch

Quiet down
   Mind your manners
      Be a good girl
         It took years of chewing
         through her own cheek
         to create a gaping hole.
         One hundred crows fly from
            that hole like bats exiting a
            cave. They tear out her stitches.
            Build magnificent nests in her hair.
               She straddles a feathered back
               as they dip and twist in flight.
               Hunting for those who stitch with long
               silver needles. Relentless pleasure
            in the chase yet they finally attack.
            Peck out bulging eyes from
            wailing faces for their dinner.
      She opens her mouth wide
      laughs then softly says
      Quiet down
   Mind your manners
Be a good girl

Yonder

Me and Huck like to sneak out and lay in the yard some nights. Tonight's a good one for it. Not too hot, not too cold. No clouds in the sky at all. You can see them hills on the moon plain as day! Kinda look like those moles Grandpap had on his arms only bigger.

The stars are so big and bright I might just pull one outta the sky and pop it in my mouth like a gumball. It probly taste like fresh spun cotton candy. I bet I could blow a giant bubble with a star gumball! If you lay on your back in the yard and stare at the sky long enough you can see them stars line up in the shape of animals and people. Mama says there's even a dragonfly in the sky, but I can't never seem to find it.

Them cadas sure are loud tonight. Sittin on them trees callin for their mate. You know if you touch the tree they will just stop and sit quiet as can be. Me and Petey usta take turns runnin and touchin the tree trunks. I wonder if heaven has cadas. Seems like it should since they don't hurt nobody.

I been tryin to take some deep breaths like Mama says I should. It kinda feels like someone is squeezin me though. Tight round my chest. Mama says we carry all our worries in our heart. When our heart gets too full we can't breathe. She says takin some good breaths in and out will push those worries right outta ya. Sumtimes I hear Huck take some good breaths when he plops down. Ummmff. I guess his heart gets full sumtimes too.

Huck's snorin. That dog can sleep anywhere, anytime. He can sleep upside down on a rock. He can sleep tucked together like a bed bug. He can even sleep standin up if he's tired nuf. He's a good boy. I love him just as much as I did Daisy. There's nuf room in your soul to love lots of people. Lots of animals. Granny Faye told me the more you love the brighter your soul shines. She said people with bright souls won't have no problem gettin into heaven. God can see how bright your soul is even fore you get to heaven. He keeps an eye on this earthly plain as best he can but he's got a lot to take care of. That's why we're supposed to keep watch on our friends and neighbors. You, know, be kind and help em out when they need it. God don't have time ta do everythin for everybody.

Mama seems to be doin pretty good. Still skinny but not as tired. I wish she would open her eyes up and see that Daddy ain't changed a bit. He's just playin games I think. Actin all nice and sweet. Course I could be wrong. The leaves on the trees change color every year, I guess people can change their ways too. I just don't want him round here. I can't help it. I've tried and tried to be forgivin like Pastor John says I should. But it just ain't happenin. I guess my soul ain't shinin too bright these days. I sure hope God gives me some more time to work it all out fore he decides if I can get inta heaven. I sure would like to be able ta see Granny and Grandpap and Petey and Daisy again.

Notebook

Last night I dreamed I was a crow
Dark as the midnight sky

Cawin from a bare tree
"Look at me, look at me!"

Then I saw myself in a broke mirror
That was hangin in that tree

I weren't no black crow
I was a nasty turkey vulture

Had a big ol dead squirrel
Hangin outta my mouth

Woke up
Got me a drink of cold milk

Resurrection

body breaking

down
down
down

grieving for all she once was

caterpillar's weeps morph into sobs transform into wails

encased
encrusted
entombed
in uncertainty

moments turn to hours become days evolve to weeks

she
winces
writhes
whimpers
uncontrollably

caterpillar resigns herself to certain death

it is in
that instant
of complete surrender

she discovers she can fly

Reawakenin

I'm sure that's Daddy's voice in the livin room. He and Mama been talkin low for sumtime. I been layin here listenin. I can hear most every word they been sayin. Things like, "this here is my house and I wanta move back in." Words like, "I can't have no drinkin in this house. This is a house of the Lord."

I think I should go peep outta the door but I'm scared. Scared I'm gonna wake my Girl up. Nuthin good would come from that. Nuthin good at all. So I lay my head down on the quilt, just barely touchin her foot with my nose. She starts stirrin a bit.

I hear footsteps on the floor. Mama's comin. I make my eyes little slits. She won't know I'm awake. She peeps in. Just a crack of the livin room lamp seeps through. She pulls the door closed. I hear her walk away.

My Girl starts stirrin a bit more. Both feet movin. A long sigh. She whispers, "Huck." I slide up to her chin. Give her a quick snuggle. Daddy's voice. Her head pops up, then she sits straight up like a pea stick. "That's Daddy." She slides outta bed quieter than a spider. Me too. We tiptoe to the door. She opens it just a crack. Mama and Daddy are sittin on the couch. Daddy has a cigarette tween his lips. Mama has her hair tied up with that long yella ribbon. Mama's drinkin coffee, Daddy has a sody pop. Daddy says, "I ain't drinkin no more. You're my wife and I'm the Girl's Daddy. I belong in this house." Mama gets up with her coffee cup and heads to the kitchen. "I know I'm your wife. I know that's your Girl in the other room. But I ain't sure you can be kind to us these days."

Daddy gets up and follows her inta the kitchen. My Girl pulls the door open just a bit more. I hear Mama set her coffee cup down. "I think you best be going fore we wake up the Girl. She ain't ready for us to be a family again."

Daddy says, "I don't care if she's ready or not. I'm ready. I'm the man of this house and it's my decision." Daddy's voice is fulla spirit. Mama says, "Now don't be raisin your voice. You'll wake her up and we can't be talkin all mean to each other." The coffee cup musta fell in the sink. The spoon hit the floor, I'm sure of it.

"I ain't talkin mean, I'm just tellin ya how it's gonna be. I been patient. I been goin to church just like you asked. I been prayin most every night out there at my boy's grave. I'm movin back inta this house." Daddy walks back inta the livin room. Mama is right behind him.

Mama says, "You ain't movin back in here yet. It ain't the right time." I hear my Girl's breath changin. I hear her heart beatin faster. Daddy turns to Mama and grabs her arm, says "I am movin back in. It is time." Mama tries to pull her arm away but Daddy won't let her. I feel my Girl startin to stir. "Let goah my arm!" Mama pulls her arm but Daddy pushes her down on the couch. My Girl nudges the door open. She steps outta the bedroom. Nuthin goods gonna come from that I'd say. Nuthin good at all.

*let go of my mama girl go back to bed get offa my mama don't
talk to me that way girl it's time for you to leave let me go
pushing slapping i gotta help mama i run for daddy's leg stop
huck mama falls got daddy's leg yellin growlin kickin mama's
hair kickin tossed against the wall oh my belly my girl has the
sody pop bottle i can't get up throws it at daddy mama runs
yellow ribbon falls to the floor handful of girls hair i can't get
up my belly hurts my girl is cryin lamp crashes daddy yellin
mama is gone daddy is pullin hair growlin gotta get to my
girl can't move she's in the floor i'm comin girl daddy kicks
again mama's back daddy's gun daddy's gun daddy's gun girl
is yellin huck huck huck i can't see no more mama has daddy's
gun nuthin goods gonna come from that nuthin good at all let
go of the girl kickin slappin let go of the girl i can't see no more
where is my girl mama girl daddy's gun huck huck huck huck
huck huck nothing good at all huck*

Notebook

He's buried next to the big
Oak with them boy babies.
Mama said that was the best
place for him to spend eternity.

She said "All good boys are buried there."

There's been a crow sittin in the
front yard goin on four days now.

• *Wendy Jett*

Acknowledgments

A big thank you to all the readers who have supported Girl's story! I am humbled and honored by your generosity and kindness.

A special thanks to Gay Herrin, Kathleen Gregg and Marcia Thornton Jones, for their time and energy in keeping Girl alive and kickin!

To Katerina Stoykova, I open my heart and give you the contents. Thank you dear one.

Please note: a version of "Grief" appeared in LexPoMo 2022.

About the Author

Wendy Jett is a longtime fitness instructor, decoupage nerd, improv junkie and loves to write. She is a born and raised Kentucky girl who now calls Lexington home. Mom to two humans, Kayla and Stevie, and one canine, Lola Jolene, she does the best she can every day! Some days she does better than others. Rumor has it that she can be bribed with peanut M&M's.

Sumthin Extra

Ms. Verna's Apple Butter

3 lb apples (peel em, core em, slice em)
¾ C water
3 C white sugar
2 tea cinnamon
1-2 pinches of nutmeg
1 pinch all spice
1 pinch salt
1 pinch cloves (Mama says Ms. Verna really puts 2 pinches in)

Cook slow on the stove or in a slow cooker for 11 hours

Dip out the apples, put em in a bowl and smash em down with a tater smasher
Smash em real good, if they get dry put some of the apple juice from the slow cooker on them

You can jar the apple butter and put in the fridge or you can go ahead and make the stack cake.

Ms. Verna's Famous Stack Cake

1¼ C butter
4 C flour
1 C white sugar
1 TB baking powder
1 TB cinnamon
1 TB ginger
1 pinch of all spice

3 big eggs
1 C buttermilk
1 C sorghum
2 pinches salt
2 tea vanilla

3 or 4 9 inch pans and some parchment paper
Whip the eggs first, then put all the wet ingredients together
Stir in the dry ingredients, it will be thick
Put the parchment paper in the bottom of the pans
Grease up the sides of the pan with some extra butter
Pour it all into the pans and smooth it out
Bake about 15 minutes at 350 degrees til dry

Cool it on a pie rack then take em outta the pan and wrap em up tight or start stacking

Cake, apple butter, cake, apple butter, cake, apple butter, cake (don't put apple butter on the top)
Be sure to put you a good bit of apple butter between them stacks

Sprinkle you some powdered sugar on the top of the cake, let it fall down the side

Slow melt you 10 caramels on the stove, then drizzle em over the top of the cake

Leather Britches

Green Beans
Salt
Water
Twine

Thread beans on twine. Don't break the beans. Put one or two meals worth on each string. Then you put the beans in ½ cup coarse salt and one gallon of water. Soak em for bout 15 minutes. This will keep them bugs from getting your beans. Then you let em drain and dry on some old newspaper or brown paper sacks. Dry em good. Hang the string up in a dry place like your porch or shed or barn for bout 3 weeks or more.

Salt and Pepper
Lard or Bacon Grease

When you wanna cook the beans pour lots of boiling water over the beans then soak em overnight. In the mornin wash em good and cover in a pan with clean water. Cook em for at least 2 hours then add the salt, pepper and lard or bacon grease. Cook bout 2 more hours. Eat em with some good crunchy skillet cornbread.